Traditional Homemade British Recipes

Soup Maker

recipe book

Sophia Hobbs

CONTENTS

Traditional, British, homemade recipes for your soup maker. A delicious collection of classic, everyday soups suitable for all soup machines, blenders and kettles... with *no need to sauté!*

You may have already enjoyed my first best-selling Soup Maker Recipe Book. Now you can extend your collection of tasty recipes with these no-fuss British soups like Cream of Chicken, Lentil & Bacon, Pea & Mint, Mulligatawny and Broccoli & Stilton Soup.

My Soup Maker & Recipes

<u>Choosing Your Ingredients</u>
Each recipe in this soup book has been written and tested in the UK, using everyday ingredients available in all UK supermarkets and written in UK measurements. There are no exotic, fancy or unique recipes – just really tasty, everyday soups. Plus, you don't have to sauté ingredients prior to making these recipes in your soup maker machine. So, with or without a sauté function on your device, these are the perfect recipes for you and your soup maker!

You'll notice sometimes I opt for tinned or ready-made ingredients, like pre-cooked rice or tinned tomatoes rather than fresh tomatoes; this is to keep things simple and fuss-free. If you have plenty of time on your hands, feel free to make things from scratch or substitute in fresh versions if you wish.

Also, sometimes I'll mention fresh herbs rather than dried herbs and vice versa. Don't let any of this stop you if you don't have the exact ingredients to hand. Dried herbs can usually be substituted for fresh herbs and vice versa, just be careful not to overdo it as dried herbs generally have a more concentrated flavour. You'll notice garlic features in many of the soup recipes included in this book. Garlic is widely used as it imparts a distinctive taste and depth to the soup; if, however, you are not a fan of garlic, consider reducing the amount in the recipe or experiment with other herbs and spices to suit your taste.

I have tried to keep all the ingredients simple and easy to work with. For example, rather than saying 200g of potatoes, I have listed it as a medium potato. If your potato is 180g or 220g it really doesn't matter, it's just a general guide to a rough weight measurement. To follow is a list of the average weights of many of the ingredients I use:

1 butternut squash 500g	**1 leek 200g**	**1 medium carrot 150g**
1 pumpkin 500g	**1 broccoli head 350g**	**1 cauliflower head 600g**
1 medium potato 200g	**1 courgette 200g**	**1 swede 600g**
1 medium sweet potato 300g	**1 medium parsnip 180g**	
1 medium onion 180g	**1 aubergine 250g**	

Using Your Soup Maker

I used a Morphy Richards 1.6 Litre Soup Maker to test our recipes. This makes approx. 4 servings (more if you're using mugs). You may have a different machine but don't worry, that's OK. You can still use the recipes but may need to make some minor adjustments, such as reducing quantities of ingredients if you have a smaller capacity soup maker. If your device does not use pre-programmed cooking settings then you should follow the manufacturer's instructions regarding cooking times. As a guide, a Morphy Richards 1.6L machine cooks for 21 minutes for a smooth soup and 28 minutes for chunky.

Some soup makers have the option to sauté ingredients. All my recipes are written with no requirement to sauté any ingredient prior to cooking, so if your machine does not have a sauté function then these are the perfect recipes for you and your soup maker.

Sautéing does, however, have its place when making some soups, intensifying the flavours of some ingredients to make a richer more flavoursome soup. So, for those who want to take the time to sauté some ingredients on the stove prior to adding to the soup maker, go ahead and sauté any onions, garlic, leeks and celery in a little olive oil for a few minutes first. If, however, a one-pot, cook-and-go soup is what you're looking for, I've got you covered!

Please note that only pre-cooked meats and fish can be used in your soup maker. Do not use raw meat or fish ingredients.

Perhaps the most important factor to adhere to when using your soup maker is never to go past the maximum fill line indicated on the machine jug or go below the minimum. These guides are there for a reason and will prevent the danger of the soup maker's hot ingredients spilling out, or the heating element burning out due to insufficient liquid. The Morphy Richards machine is equipped with an automatic cut off which prevents the blade from turning should the max line be exceeded. For this reason, each recipe advises stock quantity within a range e.g. 600-800ml and as one of the final ingredients to be added to your soup maker (before any pre-cooked items or garnish). This will allow for differing weights and sizes of other ingredients e.g. a medium potato and will ensure you don't exceed the maximum fill line. It also allows you to have a little control over the consistency of your soup.

I have indicated the consistency mode (smooth/chunky) for each recipe; however, this is a personal preference. If you prefer a smooth consistency where chunky is stated, just choose the appropriate setting on your soup maker or select the blend mode at the end of cooking to alter the final consistency. That's the beauty of how versatile soup and your soup maker can be! The chunky mode on Morphy Richards soup makers (and most other manufacturers) allows the ingredients to be heated for longer to ensure the chunky ingredients are fully cooked. For chunky soup there is no blending process, just heating; it is therefore best to cut any vegetables into small dice-sized pieces. If your soup is a little too chunky after cooking, select the blend function to achieve the desired consistency.

Some soup maker models have a pause function to allow you to remove the lid and add ingredients which may require less cooking time than set by the pre-programed modes or to allow you to check seasoning. If your soup maker doesn't have this functionality don't worry, you can add any extras at the end and warm through.

Some soup makers also have a 'clean' function to help with any stubborn ingredients that may have stuck to the heating plate of your device. This option can be handy for cleaning, however filling the jug of the machine to soak in a little hot water with washing up liquid will do just as well. Do not immerse the whole machine in water. You will find that unfortunately on occasion some ingredients will catch and burn on the heating plate and sometimes this can cause the program to stop. Making sure the ingredients are not too large and stirring the contents can help prevent this.

Please make sure you read all the manufacturer's instructions and guidelines before using your soup maker. Because soup makers are relatively simple machines, the instructions are not lengthy and will give you some helpful tips to get the best from your device.

Stock/Beware of Salt

Stock is an essential base for a great tasting soup. There are two options:
- Shop-bought stock. Either cubes/bouillon powder or fresh stock in the chilled section of a supermarket
- Homemade stock

Either will make a great soup and obviously a shop-bought option is far easier and works in perfect tandem with the fuss-free nature of making soup in a soup machine. Homemade stock, however, is preferred by some and can add an extra depth of taste to your soup. I've included 4 basic and easy stock recipes at the end of this book that you could try. They can all be made in batches and frozen for easy use when you need them.

A word of warning when using shop-bought stock or bouillon powder is to check the levels of salt. Often overuse of salt can be the main cause of a ruined soup, particularly if you also add additional seasoning, not to mention the negative health consequences of consuming more than the maximum daily recommended salt intake (6mg per day for adults). Try to check the ingredient list of stock cubes and powders and opt for ones that contain reduced levels. Look out for brands that have started selling 'zero salt' stock cubes.

If in doubt, opt for a less concentred mix of stock cube to water when making your soup. Remember that additional seasoning can be added at the end of the cooking process if needed.

I hope you enjoy this new collection of great British soups and have fun with your soup maker.

BEEF & ALE SOUP

SERVES 4
chunky

Ingredients

- 1 medium onion, chopped
- 2 medium carrots, chopped
- 1 garlic clove, sliced
- 1 celery stalk, sliced
- 1tbsp Worcestershire sauce
- 2tbsp tomato puree
- 1tsp dried thyme
- 500-600ml beef stock
- 200ml ale
- 300g cooked roast beef, chopped

Method

ONE
Add all the ingredients, except the beef, to your soup maker - making sure you do not go past the maximum fill line.

TWO
Combine well with a wooden spoon. Place the lid on the jug and select the chunky setting.

THREE
Once the cycle has finished, gently stir in the beef and warm through. Alternatively, if your soup maker has a pause function, three minutes before the end of the cooking time you can pause and add the beef.

FOUR
When the soup is ready, check the seasoning and serve.

CHICKEN SOUP

SERVES 4
chunky

Ingredients

- 1 medium carrot, chopped
- 1 medium onion, chopped
- 1 medium potato, cubed
- 1 garlic clove, sliced
- 1 celery stalk, sliced
- 1tsp dried thyme
- 100g tinned sweetcorn, drained
- 100g green beans, chopped
- 600-800ml chicken stock
- 300g cooked chicken, shredded

Method

ONE
Add all the ingredients, except the chicken, to your soup maker - making sure you do not go past the maximum fill line.

TWO
Combine well with a wooden spoon. Place the lid on the jug and select the chunky setting.

THREE
Once the cycle has finished, gently stir in the chicken and warm through. Alternatively, if your soup maker has a pause function, three minutes before the end of the cooking time you can pause and add the chicken.

FOUR
When the soup is ready, check the seasoning and serve.

CREAM OF CHICKEN SOUP

SERVES 4
●smooth

Ingredients

- 300g cooked chicken, shredded
- 1 medium carrot, chopped
- 1 medium leek, sliced
- 1 medium potato, cubed
- 1 garlic clove, sliced
- 1 celery stalk, sliced
- 1tsp dried rosemary
- 500-600ml chicken stock
- 200ml double cream

Method

ONE
Add all the ingredients, except the cream, to your soup maker - making sure you do not go past the maximum fill line.

TWO
Combine well with a wooden spoon. Place the lid on the jug and select the smooth setting.

THREE
Once the cycle has finished, gently stir in the cream and warm through. Alternatively, if your soup maker has a pause function, three minutes before the end of the cooking time you can pause and add the cream.

FOUR
When the soup is ready, check the seasoning and serve.

PEA & HAM SOUP

Ingredients

- 1 medium onion, chopped
- 1 medium carrot, chopped
- 1 medium potato, cubed
- 1tsp dried thyme
- 500g frozen peas
- 600-800ml chicken stock
- 200g thick, chunky cooked ham, chopped

Method

ONE
Add all the ingredients, except the ham, to your soup maker - making sure you do not go past the maximum fill line.

TWO
Combine well with a wooden spoon. Place the lid on the jug and select the smooth setting.

THREE
Once the cycle has finished, gently stir in the ham and warm through. Alternatively, if your soup maker has a pause function, three minutes before the end of the cooking time you can pause and add the ham.

FOUR
When the soup is ready, check the seasoning and serve.

LENTIL & BACON SOUP

SERVES 4
● smooth

Ingredients

- 1 medium onion, chopped
- 1 medium carrot, chopped
- 1 celery stalk, sliced
- 1 tin (390g) lentils, rinsed
- 1tsp dried thyme
- 600-800ml beef stock
- 4 rashers cooked bacon, chopped
- 2tbsp flat leaf parsley, chopped

Method

ONE
Add all the ingredients, except the bacon and parsley, to your soup maker - making sure you do not go past the maximum fill line.

TWO
Combine well with a wooden spoon. Place the lid on the jug and select the smooth setting.

THREE
Once the cycle has finished, gently stir in the bacon and warm through. Alternatively, if your soup maker has a pause function, three minutes before the end of the cooking time you can pause and add the bacon.

FOUR
When the soup is ready, check the seasoning, sprinkle with chopped parsley and serve.

BEEF & TOMATO SOUP

SERVES 4
⊕ chunky

Ingredients

- 1 medium onion, chopped
- 2 garlic cloves, sliced
- 2 medium carrots, chopped
- 2 celery stalks, sliced
- 1tsp dried thyme
- 1 tin (400g) chopped tomatoes
- 400-600ml beef stock
- 200g cooked roast beef, chopped

Method

ONE
Add all the ingredients, except the beef, to your soup maker - making sure you do not go past the maximum fill line.

TWO
Combine well with a wooden spoon. Place the lid on the jug and select the chunky setting.

THREE
Once the cycle has finished, gently stir in the beef and warm through. Alternatively, if your soup maker has a pause function, three minutes before the end of the cooking time you can pause and add the beef.

FOUR
When the soup is ready, check the seasoning and serve.

CHICKEN & CHUNKY VEG SOUP

SERVES 4
chunky

Ingredients

- 1 medium carrot, chopped
- 1 medium onion, chopped
- 1 medium potato, cubed
- 100g frozen peas
- 1 garlic clove, sliced
- 1tbsp olive oil
- 1tsp turmeric
- 600-800ml chicken stock
- 300g cooked chicken, shredded

Method

ONE
Add all the ingredients, except the chicken, to your soup maker - making sure you do not go past the maximum fill line.

TWO
Combine well with a wooden spoon. Place the lid on the jug and select the chunky setting.

THREE
Once the cycle has finished, gently stir in the chicken and warm through. Alternatively, if your soup maker has a pause function, three minutes before the end of the cooking time you can pause and add the chicken.

FOUR
When the soup is ready, check the seasoning and serve.

TURKEY & VEG SOUP

SERVES 4
chunky

Ingredients

- 1 medium parsnip, finely chopped
- 1 medium carrot, chopped
- 1 medium onion, chopped
- 50g spinach, chopped
- 1 tin (400g) chopped tomatoes
- 1 garlic clove, sliced
- 400-600ml chicken stock
- 2tbsp smooth cranberry sauce
- 200g cooked turkey, shredded

Method

ONE
Add all the ingredients, except the turkey and cranberry sauce, to your soup maker - making sure you do not go past the maximum fill line.

TWO
Combine well with a wooden spoon. Place the lid on the jug and select the chunky setting.

THREE
Once the cycle has finished, gently stir in the turkey and cranberry sauce to warm through. Alternatively, if your soup maker has a pause function, three minutes before the end of the cooking time you can pause to add the turkey and cranberry sauce.

FOUR
When the soup is ready, check the seasoning and serve.

CHICKEN & BARLEY SOUP

SERVES 4
chunky

Ingredients

- 2 medium carrots, chopped
- 1 medium onion, chopped
- 1 garlic clove, sliced
- 1tsp dried thyme
- 200g quick-cook pearl barley
- 600-800ml chicken stock
- 300g cooked chicken, shredded

Method

ONE
Add all the ingredients, except the chicken, to your soup maker - making sure you do not go past the maximum fill line.

TWO
Combine well with a wooden spoon. Place the lid on the jug and select the chunky setting.

THREE
Once the cycle has finished, gently stir in the chicken and warm through. Alternatively, if your soup maker has a pause function, three minutes before the end of the cooking time you can pause and add the chicken.

FOUR
When the soup is ready, check the seasoning and serve.

CLEAR BEEF BROTH

Ingredients

- 500g-1kg beef bones
- 1 medium onion, chopped
- 2 garlic cloves, sliced
- 2 medium carrots, chopped
- 2 celery stalks, sliced
- 4 bay leaves
- 2tsp black peppercorns
- 600-800ml water

Do not blend the ingredients.
Use the heat setting only.

Method

ONE
Add all the ingredients to your soup maker - making sure you do not go past the maximum fill line.

TWO
Combine well with a wooden spoon. Place the lid on the jug and place on the heat only setting – no blending.

THREE
Once the cycle has finished. Strain the broth through a fine sieve into a bowl. Keep the liquid, discard the solid ingredients.

FOUR
Remove any scum from the surface, check the seasoning and serve.

COCK-A-LEEKIE

SERVES 4
⊕ chunky

Ingredients

- 2 medium leeks, sliced
- 1 medium onion, chopped
- 1 medium potato, cubed
- 1 celery stalk, sliced
- 1tsp dried thyme
- 600-800ml chicken stock
- 300g cooked chicken thighs, shredded
- 30ml double cream
- 1tbsp lemon juice

Method

ONE
Add all the ingredients, except the chicken, cream and lemon juice, to your soup maker - making sure you do not go past the maximum fill line.

TWO
Combine well with a wooden spoon. Place the lid on the jug and select the chunky setting.

THREE
Once the cycle has finished, gently stir in the chicken and warm through. Alternatively, if your soup maker has a pause function, three minutes before the end of the cooking time you can pause and add the chicken.

FOUR
When the soup is ready stir through the cream and lemon juice. Check the seasoning and serve.

CHICKEN CHOWDER

SERVES 4
● smooth

Ingredients

- 1 medium onion, chopped
- 1 medium potato, cubed
- 1 medium carrot, chopped
- 1 red pepper, chopped
- 2 garlic cloves, sliced
- 1tsp dried marjoram
- 550-750ml chicken stock
- 200g cooked chicken, shredded
- 50ml milk
- 1tbsp cornflour
- 50ml single cream
- 1tbsp lemon juice

Method

ONE
Add all the ingredients except the chicken, milk, cornflour, cream and lemon juice to your soup maker - making sure you do not go past the maximum fill line.

TWO
Combine well with a wooden spoon. Place the lid on the jug and select the smooth setting. In a separate bowl, whisk together the milk and cornflour to make a paste.

THREE
Once the cycle has finished slowly pour in the cornflour mixture and chicken while stirring the soup. Alternatively, if your soup maker has a pause function, three minutes before the end of the cooking time You can pause to add the cornflour mixture and chicken.

FOUR
When the soup is ready stir through the cream and lemon juice. Check the seasoning and serve.

CHICKEN NOODLE SOUP

SERVES 4
chunky

Ingredients

- 1 medium carrot, sliced
- 1 medium onion, chopped
- 1 medium potato, cubed
- 2 celery stalks, sliced
- 1tsp dried thyme
- 1tsp dried parsley
- 600-800ml chicken stock
- 300g cooked chicken, shredded
- 150g packet straight-to-wok noodles, roughly chopped
- 2tbsp soy sauce

Method

ONE
Add all the ingredients, except the chicken, noodles and soy sauce, to your soup maker - making sure you do not go past the maximum fill line.

TWO
Combine well with a wooden spoon. Place the lid on the jug and select the chunky setting.

THREE
Once the cycle has finished gently stir in the chicken and noodles to warm for at least a few minutes. Ensure the noodles are separated and warmed through. Alternatively, if your soup maker has a pause function, three minutes before the end of the cooking time you can pause to add the chicken and noodles.

FOUR
When the soup is ready stir through the soy sauce. Check the seasoning and serve.

BEEF & BARLEY SOUP

SERVES 4
chunky

Ingredients

- 2 medium carrots, chopped
- 2 celery stalks, sliced
- 2 garlic cloves, sliced
- 1tsp dried thyme
- 200g quick cook pearl barley
- 1tbsp Worcestershire sauce
- 1tbsp tomato puree
- 600-800ml beef stock
- 200g cooked beef, chopped

Method

ONE
Add all the ingredients, except the beef, to your soup maker - making sure you do not go past the maximum fill line.

TWO
Combine well with a wooden spoon. Place the lid on the jug and select the chunky setting.

THREE
Once the cycle has finished, gently stir in the beef and warm through. Alternatively, if your soup maker has a pause function, three minutes before the end of the cooking time you can pause and add the beef.

FOUR
When the soup is ready, check the seasoning and serve.

SCOTCH BROTH

SERVES 4
⊕ chunky

Ingredients

- 1 medium carrot, sliced
- 1 medium onion, chopped
- 1 medium potato, cubed
- 1 medium parsnip, finely chopped
- 2 celery stalks, sliced
- 1tsp dried thyme
- 1tsp dried parsley
- 600-800ml lamb or beef stock
- 200g cooked lamb, chopped

Method

ONE
Add all the ingredients, except the lamb, to your soup maker - making sure you do not go past the maximum fill line.

TWO
Combine well with a wooden spoon. Place the lid on the jug and select the chunky setting.

THREE
Once the cycle has finished, gently stir in the lamb and warm through. Alternatively, if your soup maker has a pause function, three minutes before the end of the cooking time you can pause and add the lamb.

FOUR
When the soup is ready, check the seasoning and serve.

CHICKEN & SWEETCORN SOUP

SERVES 4
chunky

Ingredients

- 2 medium carrots, chopped
- 1 medium onion, chopped
- 1 garlic clove, sliced
- 200g tinned sweetcorn, drained
- 1tsp dried thyme
- 1tsp grated ginger (optional)
- 550-750ml chicken stock
- 200g cooked chicken, shredded
- 50ml single cream
- 1tbsp soy sauce

Method

ONE
Add all the ingredients, except the chicken, cream and soy sauce to your soup maker - making sure you do not go past the maximum fill line.

TWO
Combine well with a wooden spoon. Place the lid on the jug and select the chunky setting.

THREE
Once the cycle has finished, gently stir in the chicken and warm through. Alternatively, if your soup maker has a pause function, three minutes before the end of the cooking time you can pause and add the chicken.

FOUR
When the soup is ready stir through the cream. Add a dash of soy sauce, check the seasoning and serve.

CHICKEN & MUSHROOM CHOWDER

SERVES 4
chunky

Ingredients

- 1 medium onion, chopped
- 2 medium potatoes, cubed
- 200g mushrooms, sliced
- 1 garlic clove, sliced
- 550-750ml chicken stock
- 200g cooked chicken, shredded
- 50ml milk
- 1tbsp cornflour
- 2tbsp flat leaf parsley, chopped

Method

ONE
Add all the ingredients, except the chicken, milk, cornflour and parsley to your soup maker - making sure you do not go past the maximum fill line.

TWO
Combine well with a wooden spoon. Place the lid on the jug and select the chunky setting. In a separate bowl, whisk together the milk and cornflour to make a paste.

THREE
Once the cycle has finished, add the chicken and slowly pour in the milk and cornflour mixture while stirring the soup. Alternatively, if your soup maker has a pause function, three minutes before the end of the cooking time you can pause to add the chicken and paste.

FOUR
When the soup is ready stir check the seasoning, sprinkle with parsley and serve.

LAMB & VEGETABLE SOUP

SERVES 4
chunky

Ingredients

- 2 medium carrots, chopped
- 1 medium onion, chopped
- 1 medium sweet potato, cubed
- 1 celery stalk, sliced
- 150g frozen peas
- 1tsp dried oregano
- 600-800ml lamb or beef stock
- 200g cooked lamb, chopped

Method

ONE
Add all the ingredients, except the lamb, to your soup maker - making sure you do not go past the maximum fill line.

TWO
Combine well with a wooden spoon. Place the lid on the jug and select the chunky setting.

THREE
Once the cycle has finished, gently stir in the lamb and warm through. Alternatively, if your soup maker has a pause function, three minutes before the end of the cooking time you can pause and add the lamb.

FOUR
When the soup is ready, check the seasoning and serve.

HADDOCK CHOWDER

SERVES 4
chunky

Ingredients

- 2 medium leeks, sliced
- 2 medium potatoes, cubed
- 1 medium onion, chopped
- 1 garlic clove, sliced
- 1tbsp butter
- 400-600ml fish or vegetable stock
- 300g cooked haddock
- 50ml milk
- 1tbsp cornflour
- 200ml single cream
- 2tbsp flat leaf parsley, chopped

Method

ONE
Add all the ingredients, except the haddock, milk, cornflour, cream and parsley to your soup maker - making sure you do not go past the maximum fill line.

TWO
Combine well with a wooden spoon. Place the lid on the jug and select the chunky setting. In a separate bowl, whisk together the milk and cornflour until smooth.

THREE
Once the cycle has finished, add the haddock and slowly pour in the milk and cornflour mixture while stirring the soup. Alternatively, if your soup maker has a pause function, three minutes before the end of the cooking time you can pause to add the haddock and paste.

FOUR
When the soup is ready stir in the cream. Check the seasoning, sprinkle with parsley and serve.

FISHERMAN'S SOUP

SERVES 4
chunky

Ingredients

- 2 medium carrots, chopped
- 1 medium onion, chopped
- 2 celery stalks, sliced
- 1 tin (400g) chopped tomatoes
- 1tbsp tomato puree
- 1tsp dried thyme
- 400-600ml fish or vegetable stock
- 300g cooked cod or haddock

Method

ONE
Add all the ingredients, except the fish, to your soup maker - making sure you do not go past the maximum fill line.

TWO
Combine well with a wooden spoon. Place the lid on the jug and select the chunky setting.

THREE
Once the cycle has finished, gently stir in the fish and warm through. Alternatively, if your soup maker has a pause function, three minutes before the end of the cooking time you can pause and add the fish.

FOUR
When the soup is ready, check the seasoning and serve.

PRAWN SOUP

SERVES 4
chunky

Ingredients

- 1 medium onion, sliced
- 2 medium carrots, chopped
- 1 garlic clove, sliced
- 500-600ml vegetable or fish stock
- 200ml coconut milk
- 250g cooked small prawns, chopped

Method

ONE
Add all the ingredients, except the coconut milk and prawns, to your soup maker - making sure you do not go past the maximum fill line.

TWO
Combine well with a wooden spoon. Place the lid on the jug and select the chunky setting.

THREE
Once the cycle has finished, gently stir in the coconut milk and prawns to warm through. Alternatively, if your soup maker has a pause function, three minutes before the end of the cooking time you can pause to add the coconut milk and prawns.

FOUR
When the soup is ready, check the seasoning and serve.

CURRIED CHICKEN SOUP

Ingredients

- 300g cooked chicken, shredded
- 1 medium onion, sliced
- 1 medium potato, cubed
- 2 medium carrots, chopped
- 1 garlic clove, sliced
- 1tbsp medium curry powder
- 500-600ml chicken stock
- 200ml coconut milk

Method

ONE
Add all the ingredients, except the coconut milk, to your soup maker - making sure you do not go past the maximum fill line.

TWO
Combine well with a wooden spoon. Place the lid on the jug and select the smooth setting.

THREE
Once the cycle has finished, gently stir in the coconut milk and warm through. Alternatively, if your soup maker has a pause function, three minutes before the end of the cooking time you can pause and add the coconut milk.

FOUR
When the soup is ready, check the seasoning and serve.

HAM & VEGETABLE SOUP

SERVES 4
chunky

Ingredients

- 1 medium onion, chopped
- 1 medium carrot, chopped
- 1 medium potato, cubed
- 2 garlic cloves, sliced
- 100g frozen peas
- 600-800ml chicken stock
- 200g thick, chunky cooked ham, chopped

Method

ONE
Add all the ingredients, except the ham, to your soup maker - making sure you do not go past the maximum fill line.

TWO
Combine well with a wooden spoon. Place the lid on the jug and select the chunky setting.

THREE
Once the cycle has finished, gently stir in the ham and warm through. Alternatively, if your soup maker has a pause function, three minutes before the end of the cooking time you can pause and add the ham.

FOUR
When the soup is ready, check the seasoning and serve.

MINCED BEEF & ONION SOUP

SERVES 4
chunky

Ingredients

- 2 medium onions, chopped
- 2 medium carrots, chopped
- 1 garlic clove, sliced
- 1tsp dried thyme
- 1tsp dried oregano
- 1tbsp tomato puree
- 1 tin (400g) chopped tomatoes
- 600-800ml beef stock
- 300g cooked minced beef

Method

ONE
Add all the ingredients, except the beef, to your soup maker - making sure you do not go past the maximum fill line.

TWO
Combine well with a wooden spoon. Place the lid on the jug and select the chunky setting.

THREE
Once the cycle has finished, gently stir in the beef and warm through. Alternatively, if your soup maker has a pause function, three minutes before the end of the cooking time you can pause and add the beef.

FOUR
When the soup is ready, check the seasoning and serve.

CULLEN SKINK

SERVES 4
chunky

Ingredients

- 2 medium potatoes, cubed
- 2 medium onions, chopped
- 2 garlic cloves, sliced
- 1tbsp butter
- 550-650ml fish or vegetable stock
- 400g cooked smoked haddock
- 150ml single cream
- 4 cooked bacon rashers, finely chopped

Method

ONE
Add all the ingredients, except the haddock, cream and bacon to your soup maker - making sure you do not go past the maximum fill line.

TWO
Combine well with a wooden spoon. Place the lid on the jug and select the chunky setting.

THREE
Once the cycle has finished, gently stir in the fish and cream to warm through. Alternatively, if your soup maker has a pause function, three minutes before the end of the cooking time you can pause to add the fish and cream.

FOUR
When the soup is ready, check the seasoning and serve with bacon pieces sprinkled over the top.

BEEF & GUINNESS SOUP

SERVES 4
chunky

Ingredients

- 1 medium onion, chopped
- 2 garlic cloves, sliced
- 2 medium carrots, chopped
- 2 celery stalks, sliced
- 2tbsp tomato puree
- 1tsp dried thyme
- 500-600ml beef stock
- 200ml Guinness
- 200g cooked roast beef, chopped

Method

ONE
Add all the ingredients, except the Guinness and beef, to your soup maker - making sure you do not go past the maximum fill line.

TWO
Combine well with a wooden spoon. Place the lid on the jug and select the chunky setting.

THREE
Once the cycle has finished, gently stir in the Guinness and beef to warm through. Alternatively, if your soup maker has a pause function, three minutes before the end of the cooking time you can pause to add the Guinness and beef.

FOUR
When the soup is ready, check the seasoning and serve.

CREAM OF SPINACH SOUP

SERVES 4
smooth

Ingredients

- 250g baby spinach leaves
- Pinch of ground nutmeg
- Pinch of cayenne pepper
- 1 garlic clove, sliced
- 2tbsp butter
- 1 medium potato, cubed
- 1 medium onion, chopped
- 600-700ml vegetable stock
- 100ml single cream

Method

ONE
Add all the ingredients, except the cream, to your soup maker - making sure you do not go past the maximum fill line.

TWO
Combine well with a wooden spoon. Place the lid on the jug and select the smooth setting.

THREE
Once the cycle has finished, gently stir in the cream and warm through. Alternatively, if your soup maker has a pause function, three minutes before the end of the cooking time you can pause and add the cream.

FOUR
When the soup is ready, check the seasoning and serve.

CREAM OF CELERY SOUP

SERVES 4
● smooth

Ingredients

- 6 celery stalks, sliced
- 1 garlic clove, sliced
- 1tsp dried thyme
- 2tbsp butter
- 1tbsp olive oil
- 1 medium onion, chopped
- 1 medium potato, cubed
- 550-650ml vegetable stock
- 150ml double cream

Method

ONE
Add all the ingredients, except the cream, to your soup maker - making sure you do not go past the maximum fill line.

TWO
Combine well with a wooden spoon. Place the lid on the jug and select the smooth setting.

THREE
Once the cycle has finished, gently stir in the cream and warm through. Alternatively, if your soup maker has a pause function, three minutes before the end of the cooking time you can pause and add the cream.

FOUR
When the soup is ready, check the seasoning and serve.

VEGETABLE SOUP

Ingredients

- 1 medium potato, cubed
- 2 medium carrots, chopped
- 2 celery stalks, sliced
- 1 leek, sliced
- 1 medium onion, chopped
- 1 garlic clove, peeled & sliced
- 1tsp dried thyme
- 1tsp paprika
- 600-800ml vegetable stock

Method

ONE
Add all the ingredients to your soup maker - making sure you do not go past the maximum fill line.
TWO
Combine well with a wooden spoon.
THREE
Place the lid on the jug and select the smooth setting.
FOUR
When the soup is ready, check the seasoning and serve.

TOMATO SOUP

SERVES 4
● smooth

Ingredients

- 500g ripe plum tomatoes, chopped
- 2 garlic cloves, sliced
- 1tsp dried thyme
- ½tsp salt
- 1tbsp tomato puree
- 1 medium onion, chopped
- 1tsp brown sugar
- 600-700ml vegetable stock
- 60ml single cream
- 1tbsp balsamic vinegar (optional)

Method

ONE
Add all the ingredients, except the cream and vinegar, to your soup maker - making sure you do not go past the maximum fill line.

TWO
Combine well with a wooden spoon. Place the lid on the jug and select the smooth setting.

THREE
Once the cycle has finished, gently stir in the cream and vinegar (if using) and warm through. Alternatively, if your soup maker has a pause function, three minutes before the end of the cooking time you can pause to add the cream and vinegar (if using).

FOUR
When the soup is ready, check the seasoning and serve.

PUMPKIN SOUP

Ingredients

- 500g pumpkin, peeled & chopped
- 1 medium onion, chopped
- 2 garlic cloves, sliced
- 1tsp ground cinnamon
- 1tsp ground cumin
- 500-600ml vegetable stock
- 150ml double cream

Method

ONE
Add all the ingredients, except the cream, to your soup maker - making sure you do not go past the maximum fill line.

TWO
Combine well with a wooden spoon. Place the lid on the jug and select the smooth setting.

THREE
Once the cycle has finished, gently stir in the cream and warm through. Alternatively, if your soup maker has a pause function, three minutes before the end of the cooking time you can pause and add the cream.

FOUR
When the soup is ready, check the seasoning and serve.

POTATO & PARSLEY SOUP

SERVES 4
● smooth

Ingredients

- 4 medium potatoes, cubed
- 1 garlic clove, sliced
- 1 bunch fresh flat leaf parsley, chopped
- 1 medium onion, chopped
- 2tbsp butter
- 550-650ml vegetable stock
- 150ml single cream
- ½tsp ground black pepper

Method

ONE
Add all the ingredients, except the cream and pepper, to your soup maker - making sure you do not go past the maximum fill line.

TWO
Combine well with a wooden spoon. Place the lid on the jug and select the smooth setting.

THREE
Once the cycle has finished, gently stir in the cream and warm through. Alternatively, if your soup maker has a pause function, three minutes before the end of the cooking time you can pause and add the cream.

FOUR
When the soup is ready, sprinkle over the black pepper, check the seasoning and serve.

LENTIL & TOMATO SOUP

Ingredients

- 1 tin (390g) lentils, rinsed
- ½ tin (200g) chopped tomatoes
- 1tsp dried oregano
- 1 garlic clove, sliced
- 1 medium carrot, chopped
- 1 medium onion, chopped
- 1 celery stalk, sliced
- 500-600ml vegetable stock

Method

ONE
Add all the ingredients to your soup maker - making sure you do not go past the maximum fill line.

TWO
Combine well with a wooden spoon.

THREE
Place the lid on the jug and select the smooth setting.

FOUR
When the soup is ready, check the seasoning and serve.

ENGLISH PEA SOUP

SERVES 4
● smooth

Ingredients

- 500g frozen peas
- 1tsp paprika
- 1tsp dried thyme
- 1tsp dried basil
- 1 garlic clove, sliced
- 1 medium onion, chopped
- 1tbsp olive oil
- 600-800ml vegetable stock

Method

ONE
Add all the ingredients to your soup maker - making sure you do not go past the maximum fill line.

TWO
Combine well with a wooden spoon.

THREE
Place the lid on the jug and select the smooth setting.

FOUR
When the soup is ready, check the seasoning and serve.

SPICY PARSNIP SOUP

Ingredients

- 4 medium parsnips, finely chopped
- 1 garlic clove, sliced
- 1tsp ground cumin
- 1tsp ground coriander
- ½tsp paprika
- Pinch cayenne pepper
- 1tbsp olive oil
- 1 medium onion, chopped
- 600-800ml vegetable stock

Method

ONE
Add all the ingredients to your soup maker - making sure you do not go past the maximum fill line.
TWO
Combine well with a wooden spoon.
THREE
Place the lid on the jug and select the smooth setting.
FOUR
When the soup is ready, check the seasoning and serve.

MINESTRONE SOUP

SERVES 4
chunky

Ingredients

- ½ tin (200g) mixed beans, rinsed
- ½ tin (200g) chopped tomatoes
- 1 medium courgette, chopped
- 1 medium onion, chopped
- 1 medium carrot, chopped
- 1 celery stalk, sliced
- 50g of small pasta, such as macaroni or shells
- 1tbsp olive oil
- 1 garlic clove, sliced
- 600-800ml vegetable stock

Method

ONE
Add all the ingredients to your soup maker - making sure you do not go past the maximum fill line.
TWO
Combine well with a wooden spoon.
THREE
Place the lid on the jug and select the chunky setting.
FOUR
When the soup is ready, check the seasoning and serve.

ONION SOUP

Ingredients

- 4 medium onions, chopped
- 1 medium potato, cubed
- 1tsp dried thyme
- 1 garlic clove, sliced
- 2tbsp butter
- 600-800ml vegetable stock
- 100g Cheddar cheese, grated

Method

ONE
Add all the ingredients, except the cheese, to your soup maker - making sure you do not go past the maximum fill line.

TWO
Combine well with a wooden spoon.

THREE
Place the lid on the jug and select the chunky setting.

FOUR
When the soup is ready, check the seasoning, sprinkle over the cheese and serve.

LEEK & POTATO SOUP

Ingredients

- 3 medium leeks, sliced
- 2 medium potatoes, cubed
- 4 spring onions, sliced
- 1 garlic clove, sliced
- 550-650ml vegetable stock
- 150ml milk
- 2tbsp fresh chives, chopped

Method

ONE
Add all the ingredients, except the milk and chives, to your soup maker - making sure you do not go past the maximum fill line.

TWO
Combine well with a wooden spoon. Place the lid on the jug and select the smooth setting.

THREE
Once the cycle has finished, gently stir in the milk and warm through. Alternatively, if your soup maker has a pause function, three minutes before the end of the cooking time you can pause and add the milk.

FOUR
When the soup is ready, check the seasoning, sprinkle over the chives and serve.

CARROT & CORIANDER SOUP

SERVES 4
smooth

Ingredients

- 5 medium carrots, chopped
- 1 medium onion, chopped
- 1 medium potato, cubed
- 2tbsp fresh coriander, chopped
- 1tbsp olive oil
- 600-800ml vegetable stock

Method

ONE
Add all the ingredients to your soup maker - making sure you do not go past the maximum fill line.

TWO
Combine well with a wooden spoon.

THREE
Place the lid on the jug and select the smooth setting.

FOUR
When the soup is ready, check the seasoning and serve.

BUTTERNUT SQUASH SOUP

Ingredients

- 1 butternut squash, peeled & cubed
- 1 medium onion, chopped
- 1 garlic clove, sliced
- 1tsp ground cumin
- 1tsp ground coriander
- 2tbsp olive oil
- 600-800ml vegetable stock

Method

ONE
Add all the ingredients to your soup maker - making sure you do not go past the maximum fill line.
TWO
Combine well with a wooden spoon.
THREE
Place the lid on the jug and select the smooth setting.
FOUR
When the soup is ready, check the seasoning and serve.

BROCCOLI & STILTON SOUP

SERVES 4
smooth

Ingredients

- 1 broccoli head, chopped
- 1 medium onion, chopped
- 1 medium potato, cubed
- 600-700ml vegetable stock
- 100ml single cream
- 100g Stilton cheese, crumbled

Method

ONE
Add all the ingredients, except the cream and cheese, to your soup maker - making sure you do not go past the maximum fill line.

TWO
Combine well with a wooden spoon. Place the lid on the jug and select the smooth setting.

THREE
Once the cycle has finished, gently stir in the cream and cheese to warm through. Alternatively, if your soup maker has a pause function, three minutes before the end of the cooking time you can pause and add the cream and cheese.

FOUR
When the soup is ready, check the seasoning and serve.

TOMATO & HEARTY VEG SOUP

SERVES 4
chunky

Ingredients

- 1 tin (400g) chopped tomatoes
- 2 medium carrots, chopped
- 1 medium potato, cubed
- 1 courgette, chopped
- 1 medium onion, chopped
- 1 garlic clove, sliced
- 1tsp dried basil
- 1tsp dried oregano
- 1tbsp olive oil
- 500-600ml vegetable stock

Method

ONE
Add all the ingredients to your soup maker - making sure you do not go past the maximum fill line.

TWO
Combine well with a wooden spoon.

THREE
Place the lid on the jug and select the chunky setting.

FOUR
When the soup is ready, check the seasoning and serve.

CARROT & BUTTER BEAN SOUP

SERVES 4
⊕ chunky

Ingredients

- 3 medium carrots, chopped
- 1 tin (400g) butter beans, rinsed
- 1 medium onion, chopped
- 1 garlic clove, sliced
- 1tsp ground cumin
- ½tsp ground coriander
- 2tbsp olive oil
- 600-800ml vegetable stock

Method

ONE
Add all the ingredients to your soup maker - making sure you do not go past the maximum fill line.

TWO
Combine well with a wooden spoon.

THREE
Place the lid on the jug and select the chunky setting.

FOUR
When the soup is ready, check the seasoning and serve.

MULLIGATAWNY SOUP

SERVES 4
⊛ chunky

Ingredients

- 2 medium carrots, chopped
- 1 medium parsnip, finely chopped
- 1 medium onion, chopped
- ½ tin (200g) lentils, rinsed
- 1 eating apple chopped
- 2 celery stalks, sliced
- 1 garlic clove, sliced
- 2tbsp mild curry powder
- 2tbsp olive oil
- 1tbsp tomato purée
- 1tbsp mango chutney
- 600-800ml vegetable stock

Method

ONE
Add all the ingredients to your soup maker - making sure you do not go past the maximum fill line.

TWO
Combine well with a wooden spoon.

THREE
Place the lid on the jug and select the chunky setting.

FOUR
When the soup is ready, check the seasoning and serve.

CHUNKY MUSHROOM SOUP

SERVES 4
chunky

Ingredients

- 500g mushrooms, sliced
- 2 medium onions, chopped
- 2 garlic cloves, sliced
- 1tsp dried thyme
- 2tbsp olive oil
- 600-800ml vegetable stock

Method

ONE
Add all the ingredients to your soup maker - making sure you do not go past the maximum fill line.
TWO
Combine well with a wooden spoon.
THREE
Place the lid on the jug and select the chunky setting.
FOUR
When the soup is ready, check the seasoning and serve.

LENTIL SOUP

SERVES 4
● smooth

Ingredients

- 1 tin (390g) lentils, rinsed
- 1 celery stalk, sliced
- 2 medium carrots, chopped
- 1 medium onion, chopped
- 1tsp ground cumin
- 1tsp ground coriander
- 1tsp paprika
- 600-800ml vegetable stock

Method

ONE
Add all the ingredients to your soup maker - making sure you do not go past the maximum fill line.
TWO
Combine well with a wooden spoon.
THREE
Place the lid on the jug and select the smooth setting.
FOUR
When the soup is ready, check the seasoning and serve.

PEA & MINT SOUP

Ingredients

- 400g frozen peas
- 1 medium potato, cubed
- 1 medium onion, chopped
- 1 garlic clove, sliced
- 2tbsp fresh mint, chopped
- 600-800ml vegetable stock
- 4tbsp crème fraiche
- 1 lemon, cut into wedges

Method

ONE
Add all the ingredients, except the crème fraiche and lemon, to your soup maker - making sure you do not go past the maximum fill line.

TWO
Combine well with a wooden spoon.

THREE
Place the lid on the jug and select the smooth setting.

FOUR
When the soup is ready, check the seasoning, stir the crème fraiche through each bowl and serve with a lemon wedge.

SQUASH & SWEET PEPPER SOUP

SERVES 4
● smooth

Ingredients

- 1 butternut squash, peeled & cubed
- 2 yellow peppers, sliced
- 1 garlic clove, sliced
- 1tsp dried thyme
- 500-600ml vegetable stock
- 200ml coconut milk

Method

ONE
Add all the ingredients, except the coconut milk, to your soup maker - making sure you do not go past the maximum fill line.

TWO
Combine well with a wooden spoon. Place the lid on the jug and select the smooth setting.

THREE
Once the cycle has finished, gently stir in the coconut milk and warm through. Alternatively, if your soup maker has a pause function, three minutes before the end of the cooking time you can pause and add the coconut milk.

FOUR
When the soup is ready, check the seasoning and serve.

WARMING LENTIL & VEGGIE BROTH

SERVES 4
●smooth

Ingredients

- 1 tin (390g) lentils, rinsed
- 1 medium carrot, chopped
- 1 medium potato, cubed
- 1 courgette, chopped
- 1 medium onion, chopped
- 1 garlic clove, sliced
- 1 tbsp curry powder
- 1 tbsp olive oil
- 600-800ml vegetable stock

Method

ONE
Add all the ingredients to your soup maker - making sure you do not go past the maximum fill line.
TWO
Combine well with a wooden spoon.
THREE
Place the lid on the jug and select the smooth setting.
FOUR
When the soup is ready, check the seasoning and serve.

ENGLISH FRESH HERB SOUP

Ingredients

- 4 medium potatoes, cubed
- 1 medium onion, chopped
- 1 garlic clove, sliced
- 1 small bunch fresh parsley, chopped
- 1 small bunch fresh dill, chopped
- 1 small bunch of fresh thyme, chopped
- 1tbsp olive oil
- 600-800ml vegetable stock

Method

ONE
Add all the ingredients to your soup maker - making sure you do not go past the maximum fill line.
TWO
Combine well with a wooden spoon.
THREE
Place the lid on the jug and select the smooth setting.
FOUR
When the soup is ready, check the seasoning and serve.

RED PEPPER SOUP

Ingredients

- 4 red peppers, sliced
- 2 medium onions, chopped
- 2 garlic cloves, sliced
- 1tsp dried thyme
- 2tbsp olive oil
- 600-800ml vegetable stock
- 4tbsp crème fraiche

Method

ONE
Add all the ingredients, except the crème fraiche, to your soup maker - making sure you do not go past the maximum fill line.

TWO
Combine well with a wooden spoon.

THREE
Place the lid on the jug and select the smooth setting.

FOUR
When the soup is ready, check the seasoning, stir the crème fraiche through each bowl and serve.

SPICY LENTIL SOUP

SERVES 4
smooth

Ingredients

- 1 tin (390g) lentils, rinsed
- 1 medium onion, chopped
- 1 garlic clove, sliced
- 1 red pepper, sliced
- 1tsp ground coriander
- ½tsp paprika
- ½tsp cayenne pepper
- 600-800ml vegetable stock

Method

ONE
Add all the ingredients to your soup maker - making sure you do not go past the maximum fill line.
TWO
Combine well with a wooden spoon.
THREE
Place the lid on the jug and select the smooth setting.
FOUR
When the soup is ready, check the seasoning and serve.

SPICED CARROT & PARSNIP SOUP

SERVES 4
● smooth

Ingredients

- 2 medium parsnips, finely chopped
- 2 medium carrots, chopped
- 1 garlic clove, sliced
- ½tsp ground ginger
- Pinch of ground cinnamon
- 1tsp ground cumin
- 1tsp ground coriander
- 600-700ml vegetable stock
- 100ml coconut cream

Method

ONE
Add all the ingredients, except the coconut cream, to your soup maker - making sure you do not go past the maximum fill line.

TWO
Combine well with a wooden spoon. Place the lid on the jug and select the smooth setting.

THREE
Once the cycle has finished, gently stir in the coconut cream and warm through. Alternatively, if your soup maker has a pause function, three minutes before the end of the cooking time you can pause and add the coconut cream.

FOUR
When the soup is ready, check the seasoning and serve.

TOMATO & THREE BEAN SOUP

SERVES 4
chunky

Ingredients

- 200g ripe plum tomatoes, quartered
- 1 tin (400g) mixed beans, rinsed
- 1 medium onion, chopped
- 1 garlic clove, sliced
- 1tbsp olive oil
- 1tsp paprika
- 600-800ml vegetable stock

Method

ONE
Add all the ingredients to your soup maker - making sure you do not go past the maximum fill line.

TWO
Combine well with a wooden spoon.

THREE
Place the lid on the jug and select the chunky setting.

FOUR
When the soup is ready, check the seasoning and serve.

RUSTIC ROOT VEG SOUP

SERVES 4
chunky

Ingredients

- 1 medium potato, cubed
- 1 medium carrot, chopped
- 1 medium parsnip, finely chopped
- ¼ medium turnip, finely chopped
- 1 leek or onion, sliced
- ½tsp dried thyme
- 1tbsp olive oil
- 600-800ml vegetable stock

Method

ONE
Add all the ingredients to your soup maker - making sure you do not go past the maximum fill line.
TWO
Combine well with a wooden spoon.
THREE
Place the lid on the jug and select the chunky setting.
FOUR
When the soup is ready, check the seasoning and serve.

ST. DAVID'S WELSH SOUP

SERVES 4
smooth

Ingredients

- 3 medium leeks, sliced
- 2 medium carrots, chopped
- 1 medium parsnip, finely chopped
- 1 medium potato, cubed
- ½tsp dried thyme
- ½tsp dried sage
- 500-600ml vegetable stock
- 200ml milk

Method

ONE
Add all the ingredients, except the milk, to your soup maker - making sure you do not go past the maximum fill line.

TWO
Combine well with a wooden spoon. Place the lid on the jug and select the smooth setting.

THREE
Once the cycle has finished, gently stir in the milk and warm through. Alternatively, if your soup maker has a pause function, three minutes before the end of the cooking time you can pause and add the milk.

FOUR
When the soup is ready, check the seasoning and serve.

SWEET CABBAGE SOUP

SERVES 4
chunky

Ingredients

- 1 Savoy cabbage, chopped
- 2 medium carrots, chopped
- 2 celery stalks, sliced
- 1 garlic clove, sliced
- ½tsp dried thyme
- ½tsp dried oregano
- 1tbsp olive oil
- 1tbsp honey
- 600-800ml vegetable stock

Method

ONE
Add all the ingredients to your soup maker - making sure you do not go past the maximum fill line.
TWO
Combine well with a wooden spoon.
THREE
Place the lid on the jug and select the chunky setting.
FOUR
When the soup is ready, check the seasoning and serve.

ST. PATRICK'S DAY SOUP

Ingredients

- 4 medium potatoes, cubed
- 2 medium leeks, sliced
- 100g kale, chopped
- ½tsp dried thyme
- ½tsp dried rosemary
- 1tbsp butter
- 550-650ml vegetable stock
- 100ml milk

Method

ONE
Add all the ingredients, except the milk, to your soup maker - making sure you do not go past the maximum fill line.

TWO
Combine well with a wooden spoon. Place the lid on the jug and select the smooth setting.

THREE
Once the cycle has finished, gently stir in the milk and warm through. Alternatively, if your soup maker has a pause function, three minutes before the end of the cooking time you can pause and add the milk.

FOUR
When the soup is ready, check the seasoning and serve.

TOMATO & BASIL SOUP

SERVES 4 smooth

Ingredients

- 1 tin (400g) chopped tomatoes
- 1 medium onion, chopped
- 2 garlic cloves, sliced
- 1tsp dried basil
- 1tbsp tomato puree
- 1tbsp olive oil
- ½tsp salt
- ½tsp sugar
- 600-800ml vegetable stock

Method

ONE
Add all the ingredients to your soup maker - making sure you do not go past the maximum fill line.

TWO
Combine well with a wooden spoon.

THREE
Place the lid on the jug and select the smooth setting.

FOUR
When the soup is ready, check the seasoning and serve.

CREAM OF ASPARAGUS SOUP

SERVES 4
smooth

Ingredients

- 500g asparagus, chopped
- 1 medium onion, chopped
- 1 medium potato, cubed
- 1 garlic clove, sliced
- 550-650ml vegetable stock
- 150ml double cream
- 4tbsp fresh chives, chopped

Method

ONE
Add all the ingredients, except the cream and chives, to your soup maker - making sure you do not go past the maximum fill line.

TWO
Combine well with a wooden spoon. Place the lid on the jug and select the smooth setting.

THREE
Once the cycle has finished, gently stir in the cream and warm through. Alternatively, if your soup maker has a pause function, three minutes before the end of the cooking time you can pause and add the cream.

FOUR
When the soup is ready, check the seasoning and serve with the chives sprinkled over.

BROCCOLI SOUP

SERVES 4
● smooth

Ingredients

- 1 broccoli head, chopped
- 1 medium onion, chopped
- 1 garlic clove, sliced
- ½tsp dried thyme
- 650-750ml vegetable stock
- 150ml double cream
- 1tsp paprika

Method

ONE
Add all the ingredients, except the cream and paprika, to your soup maker - making sure you do not go past the maximum fill line.

TWO
Combine well with a wooden spoon. Place the lid on the jug and select the smooth setting.

THREE
Once the cycle has finished, gently stir in the cream and warm through. Alternatively, if your soup maker has a pause function, three minutes before the end of the cooking time you can pause and add the cream.

FOUR
When the soup is ready check the seasoning and serve with a little paprika sprinkled over each bowl.

CREAM OF VEGETABLE SOUP

SERVES 4
● smooth

Ingredients

- 1 medium potato, cubed
- 1 medium carrot, chopped
- 1 celery stalk, sliced
- 1 medium onion, chopped
- 100g peas
- ½tsp dried thyme
- ½tsp dried parsley
- 500-600ml vegetable stock
- 200ml double cream

Method

ONE
Add all the ingredients, except the cream, to your soup maker - making sure you do not go past the maximum fill line.

TWO
Combine well with a wooden spoon. Place the lid on the jug and select the smooth setting.

THREE
Once the cycle has finished, gently stir in the cream and warm through. Alternatively, if your soup maker has a pause function, three minutes before the end of the cooking time you can pause and add the cream.

FOUR
When the soup is ready, check the seasoning and serve.

CAULIFLOWER SOUP

SERVES 4
● smooth

Ingredients

- 1 cauliflower head, chopped
- 1 medium onion, chopped
- 1tsp ground cumin
- 1tsp smoked paprika
- 550-650ml vegetable stock
- 150ml double cream

Method

ONE
Add all the ingredients, except the cream, to your soup maker - making sure you do not go past the maximum fill line.

TWO
Combine well with a wooden spoon. Place the lid on the jug and select the smooth setting.

THREE
Once the cycle has finished, gently stir in the cream and warm through. Alternatively, if your soup maker has a pause function, three minutes before the end of the cooking time you can pause and add the cream.

FOUR
When the soup is ready, check the seasoning and serve.

CREAMY CHESTNUT SOUP

Ingredients

- 2 packs (360g) cooked whole chestnuts
- 1 medium onion, chopped
- Pinch of dried sage
- Pinch of dried rosemary
- 550-650ml vegetable stock
- 150ml double cream

Method

ONE
Add all the ingredients, except the cream, to your soup maker - making sure you do not go past the maximum fill line.

TWO
Combine well with a wooden spoon. Place the lid on the jug and select the smooth setting.

THREE
Once the cycle has finished, gently stir in the cream and warm through. Alternatively, if your soup maker has a pause function, three minutes before the end of the cooking time you can pause and add the cream.

FOUR
When the soup is ready, check the seasoning and serve.

WATERCRESS SOUP

SERVES 4
smooth

Ingredients

- 150g watercress
- 1 medium onion, chopped
- 1 medium potato, cubed
- 1 garlic clove, sliced
- 550-650ml vegetable stock
- 150ml double cream

Method

ONE
Add all the ingredients, except the cream, to your soup maker - making sure you do not go past the maximum fill line.

TWO
Combine well with a wooden spoon. Place the lid on the jug and select the smooth setting.

THREE
Once the cycle has finished, gently stir through the cream.

FOUR
When the soup is ready, check the seasoning and serve.

SWEETCORN SOUP

Ingredients

- 1 tin (325g) sweetcorn, drained
- 1 medium onion, chopped
- 1 garlic clove, sliced
- 1 red chilli, chopped (no seeds)
- 550-650ml vegetable stock
- 150ml coconut cream

Method

ONE
Add all the ingredients, except the coconut cream, to your soup maker - making sure you do not go past the maximum fill line.

TWO
Combine well with a wooden spoon. Place the lid on the jug and select the chunky setting.

THREE
Once the cycle has finished, gently stir in the coconut cream and warm through. Alternatively, if your soup maker has a pause function, three minutes before the end of the cooking time you can pause and add the coconut cream.

FOUR
When the soup is ready check the seasoning and serve.

CREAM OF MUSHROOM SOUP

SERVES 4
smooth

Ingredients

- 500g white mushrooms, sliced
- 1 medium onion, chopped
- 2 garlic cloves, sliced
- ½tsp ground black pepper
- 2tbsp butter
- 550-650ml vegetable stock
- 150ml double cream
- 2tbsp fresh parsley, chopped

Method

ONE
Add all the ingredients, except the cream and parsley, to your soup maker - making sure you do not go past the maximum fill line.

TWO
Combine well with a wooden spoon. Place the lid on the jug and select the smooth setting.

THREE
Once the cycle has finished, gently stir in the cream and warm through. Alternatively, if your soup maker has a pause function, three minutes before the end of the cooking time you can pause and add the cream.

FOUR
When the soup is ready, check the seasoning and serve with the parsley sprinkled over the top.

CREAM OF ONION SOUP

SERVES 4
● smooth

Ingredients

- 4 medium onions, chopped
- 2 garlic cloves, sliced
- 1tsp dried rosemary
- 1tbsp olive oil
- 1tbsp butter
- 550-650ml vegetable stock
- 150ml double cream

Method

ONE
Add all the ingredients, except the cream, to your soup maker - making sure you do not go past the maximum fill line.

TWO
Combine well with a wooden spoon. Place the lid on the jug and select the smooth setting.

THREE
Once the cycle has finished, gently stir in the cream and warm through. Alternatively, if your soup maker has a pause function, three minutes before the end of the cooking time you can pause and add the cream.

FOUR
When the soup is ready, check the seasoning and serve.

LUXURY LEEK SOUP

SERVES 4
smooth

Ingredients

- 4 medium leeks, sliced
- 1 medium potato, cubed
- 1 eating apple, chopped
- 1 medium onion, chopped
- 1 garlic clove, sliced
- 1tbsp olive oil
- 500-600ml vegetable stock
- 150ml double cream
- 2tbsp fresh chives, chopped

Method

ONE
Add all the ingredients, except the cream and chives, to your soup maker - making sure you do not go past the maximum fill line.

TWO
Combine well with a wooden spoon. Place the lid on the jug and select the smooth setting.

THREE
Once the cycle has finished, gently stir in the cream and warm through. Alternatively, if your soup maker has a pause function, three minutes before the end of the cooking time you can pause and add the cream.

FOUR
When the soup is ready, check the seasoning, sprinkle over the chives and serve.

CREAM OF TOMATO SOUP

SERVES 4
● smooth

Ingredients

- 500g ripe plum tomatoes, chopped
- 1 medium onion, chopped
- 1 garlic clove, sliced
- 2tbsp olive oil
- 2tbsp cream cheese
- 1tsp dried oregano
- 500-600ml vegetable stock
- 200ml single cream

Method

ONE
Add all the ingredients, except the cream , to your soup maker - making sure you do not go past the maximum fill line.

TWO
Combine well with a wooden spoon. Place the lid on the jug and select the smooth setting.

THREE
Once the cycle has finished, gently stir in the cream and warm through. Alternatively, if your soup maker has a pause function, three minutes before the end of the cooking time you can pause and add the cream.

FOUR
When the soup is ready, check the seasoning and serve.

KALE SOUP

Ingredients

- 400g kale, chopped
- 1 medium onion, chopped
- 1 medium potato, cubed
- 1 garlic clove, sliced
- 1tsp dried thyme
- 500-600ml vegetable stock
- 200ml single cream

Method

ONE
Add all the ingredients, except the cream, to your soup maker - making sure you do not go past the maximum fill line.

TWO
Combine well with a wooden spoon. Place the lid on the jug and select the smooth setting.

THREE
Once the cycle has finished, gently stir in the cream and warm through. Alternatively, if your soup maker has a pause function, three minutes before the end of the cooking time you can pause and add the cream.

FOUR
When the soup is ready, check the seasoning and serve.

SWEET POTATO SOUP

Ingredients

- 3 medium sweet potatoes, cubed
- 1 medium onion, chopped
- 1 garlic clove, sliced
- 1tsp ground cumin
- 1tsp ground coriander
- 550-650ml vegetable stock
- 150ml coconut milk
- 1/2tsp ground black pepper

Method

ONE
Add all the ingredients, except the coconut milk and pepper, to your soup maker - making sure you do not go past the maximum fill line.

TWO
Combine well with a wooden spoon. Place the lid on the jug and select the smooth setting.

THREE
Once the cycle has finished, gently stir in the coconut milk and warm through. Alternatively, if your soup maker has a pause function, three minutes before the end of the cooking time you can pause and add the coconut milk.

FOUR
When the soup is ready, sprinkle over the black pepper, check the seasoning and serve.

SPROUT SOUP

SERVES 4
• smooth

Ingredients

- 400g Brussels sprouts, halved
- 1 medium onion, chopped
- 2 medium carrots, chopped
- 1tsp dried rosemary
- 1tbsp butter
- 550-650ml vegetable stock
- 150ml single cream

Method

ONE
Add all the ingredients, except the cream, to your soup maker - making sure you do not go past the maximum fill line.

TWO
Combine well with a wooden spoon. Place the lid on the jug and select the smooth setting.

THREE
Once the cycle has finished, gently stir in the cream and warm through. Alternatively, if your soup maker has a pause function, three minutes before the end of the cooking time you can pause and add the cream.

FOUR
When the soup is ready, check the seasoning and serve.

TOMATO & FENNEL SOUP

Ingredients

- 1 tin (400g) chopped tomatoes
- 1 fennel bulb, chopped
- 1 medium onion, chopped
- 2 garlic cloves, sliced
- 1tsp paprika
- 400-600ml vegetable stock

Method

ONE
Add all the ingredients to your soup maker - making sure you do not go past the maximum fill line.

TWO
Combine well with a wooden spoon.

THREE
Place the lid on the jug and select the smooth setting.

FOUR
When the soup is ready, check the seasoning and serve.

CAULIFLOWER CHEESE SOUP

SERVES 4
smooth

Ingredients

- 1 medium onion, chopped
- 1 garlic clove, sliced
- 1 celery stalk, sliced
- 2tbsp butter
- 1 medium cauliflower head, chopped
- ½tsp paprika
- Pinch of nutmeg
- 600-800ml vegetable stock
- 150g Cheddar cheese, grated
- 2tbsp fresh chives, chopped

Method

ONE
Add all the ingredients, except the cheese and chives, to your soup maker - making sure you do not go past the maximum fill line.

TWO
Combine well with a wooden spoon. Place the lid on the jug and select the smooth setting.

THREE
Once the cycle has finished, gently stir in the cheese to melt. Alternatively, if your soup maker has a pause function, three minutes before the end of the cooking time you can pause and add the cheese.

FOUR
When the soup is ready, check the seasoning and serve with chopped chives.

MUSHROOM & BARLEY SOUP

SERVES 4 chunky

Ingredients

- 400g mushrooms, sliced
- 1 medium carrot, chopped
- 1 medium onion, chopped
- 2 garlic cloves, sliced
- 1tsp dried thyme
- 200g quick cook pearl barley
- 1tsp olive oil
- 600-800ml vegetable stock
- 2tbsp fresh flat leaf parsley, chopped

Method

ONE
Add all the ingredients, except the parsley, to your soup maker - making sure you do not go past the maximum fill line.

TWO
Combine well with a wooden spoon.

THREE
Place the lid on the jug and select the chunky setting.

FOUR
When the soup is ready, check the seasoning and serve with chopped parsley sprinkled over the top.

CREAM OF ARTICHOKE SOUP

SERVES 4
• smooth

Ingredients

- 500g frozen artichoke hearts
- 1 medium potato, cubed
- 1 medium onion, chopped
- 2tbsp olive oil
- 2 garlic cloves, sliced
- 500-600ml vegetable stock
- 200ml single cream

Method

ONE
Add all the ingredients, except the cream, to your soup maker - making sure you do not go past the maximum fill line.

TWO
Combine well with a wooden spoon. Place the lid on the jug and select the smooth setting.

THREE
Once the cycle has finished, gently stir in the cream and warm through. Alternatively, if your soup maker has a pause function, three minutes before the end of the cooking time you can pause and add the cream.

FOUR
When the soup is ready, check the seasoning and serve.

CARROT & ORANGE SOUP

Ingredients

- 4 medium carrots, chopped
- 2 medium leeks, sliced
- 1 medium potato, cubed
- 1tbsp butter
- 600-800ml vegetable stock
- 4tbsp orange juice

Method

ONE
Add all the ingredients, except the orange juice, to your soup maker - making sure you do not go past the maximum fill line.

TWO
Combine well with a wooden spoon.

THREE
Place the lid on the jug and select the smooth setting.

FOUR
When the soup is ready stir through the orange juice, check the seasoning and serve.

VEGETABLE STOCK

Ingredients

- 1tbsp olive oil
- 1 medium onion, chopped
- 2 medium carrots, chopped
- 1 medium leek, sliced
- 2 celery stalks, sliced
- 3 garlic cloves, sliced
- 1tsp thyme
- 1tbsp black peppercorns
- 2 bay leaves
- 1tsp salt
- 3litres water

Method

ONE
Heat the olive oil in a saucepan and gently sauté the onions, carrots, leeks, celery, garlic and thyme for a few minutes.

TWO
Add the remaining ingredients and bring to the boil. Leave to gently simmer for 30 minutes with a lid on.

THREE
Allow to cool for a little while. Pour the stock into a bowl through a sieve to separate the solid ingredients. Discard the contents of the sieve.

FOUR
Store the stock in the fridge for a day or two or freeze in batches.

CHICKEN STOCK

Ingredients

- 1tbsp olive oil
- 2 medium onions, chopped
- 2 medium carrots, chopped
- 2 celery stalks, sliced
- 1 leftover roast chicken carcass
- 2 bay leaves
- 1tsp dried thyme
- 1tsp salt
- 1tsp black peppercorns
- 3litres water

Method

ONE
Heat the olive oil in a saucepan and gently sauté the onions, carrots and celery for a few minutes.

TWO
Add the remaining ingredients and bring to the boil. Leave to gently simmer for 30 minutes with the lid on.

THREE
Allow to cool for a little while. Pour the stock into a bowl through a sieve to separate the solid ingredients. Discard the contents of the sieve.

FOUR
Store the stock in the fridge for a day or two or freeze in batches.

FISH STOCK

Ingredients

- 1tbsp olive oil
- 2 medium onions, chopped
- 3 medium carrots, chopped
- 1 celery stalk, sliced
- 1 leek, sliced
- 1tbsp black peppercorns
- 1tsp dried thyme
- 500g fish bones, heads, carcasses etc
- 1tsp salt
- 3litres water

Method

ONE
Heat the olive oil in a saucepan and gently sauté the onions, carrots, celery and leeks for a few minutes.

TWO
Add the remaining ingredients and bring to the boil. Leave to gently simmer for 30 minutes with the lid on.

THREE
Allow to cool for a little while. Pour the stock into a bowl through a sieve to separate the solid ingredients. Discard the contents of the sieve.

FOUR
Store the stock in the fridge for a day or two or freeze in batches.

BEEF STOCK

Ingredients

- 1tbsp olive oil
- 2 medium onions, chopped
- 2 medium carrots, chopped
- 2 celery stalks, sliced
- 3 garlic cloves, sliced
- 1tbsp black peppercorns
- 2 bay leaves
- 1tsp dried thyme
- 1kg beef bones
- 1tsp salt
- 3litres water

Method

ONE
Heat the olive oil in a saucepan and gently sauté the onions, carrots, celery and garlic for a few minutes.

TWO
Add the remaining ingredients and bring to the boil. Leave to gently simmer for 30 minutes with the lid on.

THREE
Allow to cool for a little while. Pour the stock into a bowl through a sieve to separate the solid ingredients. Discard the contents of the sieve.

FOUR
Store the stock in the fridge for a day or two or freeze in batches.

GARLIC CROUTONS

Ingredients

- 3tbsp melted butter
- 4 slices stale thick bread, cut into bite size cubes
- 4 garlic cloves, minced
- Salt & pepper

Method

ONE
Preheat the oven to 180C/Gas 5.

TWO
In a large bowl combine all the ingredients together to completely coat the bread.

THREE
Place on a baking tray and bake for 8-10 minutes or until crispy and golden brown.

FOUR
Store in an airtight container for up to 5 days.

SEEDY CIABATTA CROUTONS

SERVES 4
oven-baked topping

Ingredients

- 4tbsp olive oil
- 1 small stale ciabatta loaf, cut into bite size cubes
- 2tbsp mixed seeds (poppy, sunflower, sesame seeds etc)
- Salt & pepper

Method

ONE
Preheat the oven to 180C/Gas 5.

TWO
In a large bowl combine all the ingredients together to completely coat the bread. Use your fingers to press the seeds into the bread so they stick.

THREE
Place on a baking tray and bake for 8-10 minutes or until crispy and golden brown.

FOUR
Store in an airtight container for up to 5 days.

CRISPY ONION SOUP TOPPER

Ingredients

- 3 medium onions, sliced thinly
- 65g plain flour
- ½tsp salt
- ½tsp paprika
- Pinch of black pepper
- Vegetable oil for frying

Method

ONE
In a shallow bowl mix together the flour, salt, black pepper, and paprika. Add the onions and combine to completely coat the onions.

TWO
Heat about 2cm of vegetable oil in a heavy-bottomed frying pan over medium-high heat.

THREE
Carefully place the onions in the hot oil, being careful not to overcrowd the pan. Fry for 3-4 minutes, stirring occasionally, until they are golden brown and crispy.

FOUR
Transfer the onions to a plate with kitchen roll to absorb any excess oil. Serve the crispy fried onions as a soup topper.

ROASTED CHICKPEA SOUP TOPPER

SERVES 4
oven-baked topping

Ingredients

- 1tbsp olive oil
- 1 tin chickpeas (400g) drained and rinsed
- ½tsp garlic powder
- 1tsp paprika
- Salt & pepper

Method

ONE
Preheat the oven to 200C/Gas 6.

TWO
In a large bowl combine all the ingredients together to completely coat the chickpeas.

THREE
Place on a baking tray in a single layer and bake for 20-25 minutes or until crispy and golden brown.

FOUR
Remove from the oven and allow to cool before using as a crunchy soup topper.

Printed in Great Britain
by Amazon